Bones in the Octagon

Bones in the Octagon

CAROLYN McCURDIE

m

A catalogue record for this book is available from the
National Library of New Zealand.

ISBN 978-0-9941172-1-2

2015 series ISBN 978-0-9941172-4-3

Series editor: Mary McCallum
Series design: William Carden-Horton
Typeset & internal design: Paul Stewart

Printed by Wakefields Digital,
Wellington, New Zealand

First published in 2015 as part of
the Mākaro Press Hoopla series

m

Mākaro Press
PO Box 41-032 Eastbourne 5047
makaropress@gmail.com
makaropress.co.nz

Our books speak for themselves

Contents

In loving memory of

Bill McCurdie 1915–1995
Dorothy McCurdie 1919–2011

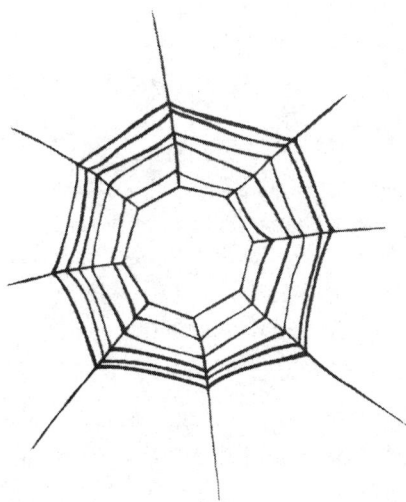

south/hoopla

Inside a story

Once, a young man imagined a future
of alpine grandeur. Purple and gold.
To begin, he set up a stall in the main street
selling fruit in brown paper bags.

Carrying her school bag, his sister arrived.
She put a chair behind him close to the wall
and sat down to read. He turned to greet her
but she was shifting one shoulder adjusting
the fall of the light on the page.

The lights changed, saying,
Cross Now.

Unending, unending, the people rushed by
from the west to the east, and the east
to the west. They wore knitted gloves
and coats with the buttons done up. He imagined
them streaming unstoppable over the western
horizon. What waits there? He imagined
the opposite stream disappearing into the sea.
Could all of them swim?

He turned to ask his sister this, but she frowned
as if touched by pain in the story. She pulled
her hair to her mouth and chewed
on deep questions.

The lights changed, saying,
Don't Cross.

Some people stopped, bought one bag or two
and smiled, the brief warmth of strangers.
And he imagined, because the population was small,
that those people arrived at the end of the street,
put on new coats and wigs and hurried
back the way they had come.
Round and round.

He turned to ask, did she think this was likely
but her face was inward with laughter. She flipped
over the page.

The lights changed, saying,
Cross Now.

A hooded woman crossed the street
to buy cherries. She paid him
in seashells, laid them out on his stall so that
light caught the shy iridescence inside
where dreams were beginning of purple
and blue and pink and gold.

This is why we went under the sea,
said the woman, to bring these
for you.

January begins

For New Year, I wish this for you:
Janus, the god who looks forward
and back, till his pupils dilate, intoxication
of distance. It's his month.

Here's the calendar photo he hangs
on your wall: salt caravans in Niger,
from a paraglider, so high that camels
seem strung as if notes on scribbled
staves of song. On the horizon, a thin
sprinkle like fire-blackened grain:
another caravan.

One way with millet to trade, the return
journey with salt. They follow the line
of the dunes, begin
in autumn, stop
before summer rains.
Those little blips are human beings,
commas, apostrophes, keeping
the line.

My wish for you: Janus, the god of
transition. Here, in these last islands
of human arrival,
the ancient journeys belong to birds.
When autumn comes, you'll stand
on the beach to watch shearwaters
day after day, low to the ocean

wings tipping the spray and the rocks
of the headlands.
Their mental map loops
the Pacific, returning in spring.

Janus, the god who lays out
mental maps. With a thumb nail
he flattens the folds. The paraglider
delights him, the long view, the old
is the new. He sings its audacity.
When you first learned to balance,
unsteady, surprised, this
was the song that he gave you.

Since then, self-mutilation
of bumper-to-bumper, the queues
in the customs hall.

Still he sings it, insists,
on your calendar, through the letters
of your name, till you play it
in your finger bones
like crystals of sunlight
that quiver down dunes
till you push out from the beach,
dance it in the arches of your feet
as they brace on wet, slanted wood,
on the slow-rising heft
of water. As they take one step.

Around and around it comes back. Can you
hear it, that song? Yes.
The intoxication of song. After rain
and when the wind shifts
to nor'west.

I wish this for you: Janus
who unlocks the doors and tells you
the world, the wide, shining world,
is open. Go through.

Memories of long grass

for Lesley and Steve

We were quick to claim this ground
relinquished by thick-tongued cows
not yet chomped by bulldozers;
on long swooping slopes and gullies
the seeding grasses nodded, waited just for us.

Disdainful, we pushed aside
stalks swaddled by the nursery web spider
ready for her teeming young;
we trampled tracks where no one
walked but skinks, mice, a cat.
Tiger tracks.

The huts we made were dreams of huts, made more
of air than granny-knotted grass that broke
and slipped. Inside the open walls, we sat
and watched the sun stripe our arms and legs.

We rolled the grass flat to make circles
the radius of our bodies. Then our eyes probed eternity
finding it blue, and beyond that, blue
and beyond that …

The grass held us cupped; the sky bent down
and sipped us up.

Invitation to dance

Walk with me.
Pack no bags.
In your mind find quiet. Even if
it's a calm you can barely remember, pack
only that, the quiet time.

You know about running, the mad-time taxi dash
to an airport
to anywhere
with night-time crazy lights that spin left
and right, and a heavy bag to grip,
to belong to.

Somewhere within panic there's always a slither,
a skid, upside down
and back to where you began.

So, walk.
Break rules.
Be naked, stripped
down to your leg bones,
your spine. Straight.
Untouched.

Don't look back.
Not for years.

Then years, and when you've found
and unfolded scraps of peace you hid
in a book or filed
among seed packets,
when those bits have been stitched
in a garment that you wear long and flowing
with an elegance unaware of itself, then
you might look.

You might stand somewhere stratospheric
where the air is so cold
it tightens your lungs, makes your eyes wet
and salt, where the far bright line of the ocean
makes distance into illusion.

You might look through your blinking to that younger
self. You might ask her: how long since you laughed?
Expect a false laugh. A denial.
While you wait, give her all that you have:
a largeness, the swirl of a cape or a skirt,
and balance at speed. Stand by her
as she pulls on her boots.

Ambush

She's walking with the wind behind her.
She's a broad-shouldered woman
and she knows she's being followed.
She spins, quick on the draw, and the street
gives back its innocent look
a look of nobody there, not even a sparrow.
She's a no-nonsense woman and she suspects
a mob of leaves, dry old rustlers, that loiter by the corner
but they mount the tarseal, round up shadows. They deny it.
She walks on. Again, she's being followed …

… by an empty cardboard box.
Dropped, she supposes, by some cowboy rubbish collector
and now herded with leaves, plastic
along the street behind her.
Pock, pocketty, on the footpath, then it stops.
As if it has something to say
or something to offer.

She continues to walk; she has somewhere to go.
She's a rational woman, her mind's filled with serious matters
but the box steals her attention.
It's small, square
as if it once held a ring, she thinks,
or some tinselled promise
or, more than likely, putty,
or garden twine
for tying up scarlet runners.
She's a practical woman.

In her mind, a picture forms,
of something cupped in satin,
with no function except
to contain the air in coils
of smooth craftedness.
Beautiful, of course,
pleased with itself
and expecting to last forever.
Pock, pock, on the footpath, the box
totters, tips, slides to the gutter.
And no matter how the woman clutches her coat
the wind aims, and finds
every dry gulch in her bones.

Dislocation

Who are you?

The streets are wet   abandoned.
Above your head the town hall clock
gongs a late   evaporating hour.

The cathedral   floats
lifted by steps
as if sketched on the sky by
a tall thin pencil.

All you want is warmth
solid ground.

From nowhere a police car rolls
its weight along dotted lines
in case this place folds   peels away in the wind.

Nobody wants to know
who you are.

The poet
with his trapped, stone eyes
gazes after   words
names
escaping.

Then rain falls aslant
through the streetlight
as if writing lines
of urgent warning.

Two boys on roller blades

They've set up a goal:
some wooden struts

wedged in the gutter, strapped
to a power pole

and a sheet of black vinyl salvaged
trimmed, for this.

They flow across the road
up and back and around

loose, lazy
as if it's the camber of the road

that lifts them, drops and lifts
till a neighbour's car in careful low gear

washes the boys to the side
in a cross-current.

Hockey sticks dangle, wait.
Then wrists flex; they check,

snag the pockmarked puck, flick it
whack it, gulp into the goal.

Circling again, no words
just eyebrows.

Power poles along the street

and yet we are trees

stripped to essentials
of stance
of grave forest quiet

our sway
our slow baritone
dry-chipped in the sawdust

not dead not alive

no entwined roots of plantation
but connected
wind in the wires

ghosts on the cusp of not-there
but here are the birds
arms wide for the birds

and not dead

when the night roars with blackness
and all things are wild
we whip and thrash
swing our lights out to the edge
of shatter
shoulder a swirling cloak of rain
to go striding
                striding

and yet

we stand in the soft
of the morning
holding the street signs
marking the bus stops

Still life

after earthquakes in Christchurch & Japan

The speed of the galaxy cannot
be known. One calculation says it flicks
through space at six hundred and thirty kilometres
each second. No fixed point exists
as a measure. Nothing is still.

A vase stands on the table.
Elegant.
Tall, blue.
Sometimes it holds
a dog-paddling jostle
of pansies that shiver
in the breeze from the window.

The galaxy rotates. The sun reels
on an outer edge at perhaps two hundred
and twenty kilometres per second.

The vase, in season, holds
hydrangeas, assured, bouffant.
Some mornings there are toast crumbs
all over the table but the vase is always
tall, blue
containment.

Around the sun the earth turns
at thirty kilometres
a second. Measured.
A wedge of earth's mantle shifts
half a metre.

Unbalance.
Sirens keening, keening. Under broken rock
a phone keeps ringing,
keeps ringing.

The idea of a vase.
Alone on a table, under
the shattered weight
of starlight.
Empty. Contours of a small,
blue centre.

Old possumers' track

Because of the weather. So still.
The sky overcast, a lull after
last night's downpour. The day waits
for rain.

Because the trees are so high. They push
the sky up, create vaulted space.
Down here nothing moves. Birds are somewhere
else in the canopy, *call-reply-call*, far off.
And further away, the resounding,
resounding of surf.
Here, no sound.

Because spider strands break across
your eyelids, your chin as you walk
down the track.
No one has been here.

Because there's no cell phone coverage.
Because you watch where you
put your feet; you locate the orange
marker on the tree in front before
you move from the marker behind.

Because the silence is vibrant.
Like when you enter a room
and conversation stops.
Because you bring a scepticism. A diffidence.
Because reasons ... you have stepped
beyond reason.

Something here untouched
never breathed on
that coalesces
to a ngiru-ngiru on a nearby
twig, scrutiny close up,
small, feathered courtesy. Then gone.
Back into gaps between
the gaps between the
gaps between the gaps between
the trees.

Sometimes the paint is still wet

Watch out,
the neighbours told us, they're wild;
they're fierce.
When you walk along the tracks
be noisy, sing,
in case you corner
a feral bull, or worse, a feral cow
with her calf.

Like a story told in the dark
to cheeky children or brash
newcomers to render them
wide-eyed and quiet.

The signs of them were clear enough:
the cowpats, the cropped
grass, the deeply pocked
mud by the creek. But
these were descendants
of the clever ones
those who evaded
muster when the farm folded
on land too dry, too steep, too far
from markets. These remnants, too,
were clever and wherever you looked,
not there.

Sometimes on a still
night the strangle-throated

shriek of a cow, defying
and breaking up sleep.

Each day I had to walk
from our back gate along tracks
through the gorse and mānuka
to the road at the top of the ridge.
One dark winter morning the long grass
near our gate was flattened,
smoothed by large nesting
bodies. When I touched the grass
it was warm. I'd seen nothing, heard
nothing.

As if just visiting.
As if painted
figures hidden in caves
for thousands of years took flesh,
came out to graze, breathe
salt air, blink
at moonlight.

In the five years living there
I saw one just once.
From the road looking down
to the bay, I watched a young male
emerge from the scrub
to eat grass near
the water. The early light

touched his horns and the hair
along his back. His head jerked up
and he held my gaze for a second before
he returned to the kānuka
shadows and
vanished.

I carry him here, painted
still on the dreaming
walls of my mind.

Not gone.

Storksbill (*erodium cicutarium*)

Across a hieroglyphed wall three green storks
have been walking for three thousand years.

With the ancient wisdom that saw kinship
in everything, the people linked this migrating bird

to the soul that left the body
in sleep, and returned in the morning.

The skies over my roof have never
held storks. But look at this little plant

and see the family likeness, spindled tangle of long
red legs, feathered green still awry as if

crash landed. Did its soaring take it too close
to the sun? Now, searching for shade

under my hedge, it kneels
in the crumbling alphabets of old leaves.

The pods explain the name. Their bird beaks lift
remembering sky, then dive into soil with the seed.

The long wait that is winter. The prayerfulness
that shelters under the frost.

Then, hello, little green-fledged souls.
Here you are again.

Tissue and comb

I

He fled the tenements of Glasgow for the Royal Navy
the instant he turned eighteen.

When I visit, we sit at the kitchen table,
he in dressing gown and slippers,
and he gets out the photos.
He picks this one out as if it's not important.
It's the navy band. I don't even know,
he says, where I am in this.
I'm not surprised; the sun creates twenty fiercely
white uniforms, all faceless under the peaks of their caps.
Just a hint of a beard or a smile at the edge of the black.

He's laughing, shy. The only thing I could play, he says,
was the tissue and comb. I wonder I had the cheek to be there.

If there was music,
Dad would find it.

2

In a city street
off-duty with other sailors,
a small boy ran to him,
took his arm, crooked it
to cradle his head.
Then ran away.

Dad describes this as you might tell
of a rare butterfly that alights
on a finger: random beauty
chooses you.

Post

Where did you go when you died?
I'm a child again, asking.

I dream you're waiting for letters.
Why does nobody write?
I dream I'm gathering a search party,
frantic, late, because you're out there somewhere
cold and knowing we'll come but
till now, we've just been so busy.

I wake from these dreams, panicked, appalled.

Then I dream two letters arrive,
blue, from a naval base.
I stand at the mail box, yelling,
Mum! Letters for you, from Dad!

Dad.

The echo comes back.
A child again, calling.

The blue and white tablecloth
for Mum

Should we throw it away?
Your fingers rub at a stain by your plate.
Not a stain. It's a hole
and I could mend it, but won't.

When the light shines through it you notice
the thinness and soon, here and here, more holes.
And see how the blue lines are worn
by the pull of connection

from my side of the table to yours,
by paths of conversation
of passing gravy, salt.
How many years have we stood

pegging it out
watching its white,
its snap-salute blue
kick high, swing, kick,

touch toes with the blue-white of sky?
This is the one that still drapes
fresh air across our table,
that smiles a picnic invitation

of lettuce from the garden,
apple from the Peasgood Nonsuch tree.
Of course we should throw it away –
but on the days when it's just me and you

we bring it out again and laugh at how silly we are.

Almost a year

It's May. From our window I watch leaves leap and skid
into drifts across the road. Those unruly
heaps used to fill you with glee, with a not-dead-yet
urge to jump, kick, plunge into their deep

prickly crunch. 'Where are the kids?' you'd say.
Today the cold wind has driven the kids inside
but on the couch the sun is so strong that the cat holds
a paw over his eyes to sleep.

A different cat. This one's a generous pudding, toffee
and cream. Our ladyship died
a few months after you. She would stare into
your empty chair and yowl.

Other vanishings. This morning I drove to the Recycle Shop
with blankets and towels I don't need.
With every removal, the old woman, frail and exasperated
by a life too long, clicks a door behind her.

Yet here you are. You're laughing and showing
us the moves from a night in your courting days –
you, Dad, your friends in a line across a wee-small-hours
London street, doing the Lambeth Walk.

Dancing girl. Arm-in-arm, strut, head-toss, kick.
With me now on this bright
leaf-wheeling afternoon.

Like living in a distant land

At night, you hear the house
creak against its emptiness,
against dry air along the hallway
no longer alive with soft syncopations
of breathing.

Half asleep, you listen to water
in the downpipe as if hearing
voices through a wall, rapid
vital conversation that denies
you even a word, never pauses for laughter,
never subsides to start stacking plates.

In those days
who you were:
daughter, wife, mother,
clear in their intonations
of your name.

In the morning there are cows as usual
on the hill across the valley.
They stand in file along a fenceline
spaced out so neatly they remind
you of stitching that holds together the edge
of a blanket. Then
they move, bunch, straggle.

Can you hear this?

I stood
on a headland above a wide, sunlit bay
empty of all but dunes and long rolling surf,
of all but its ancient self.

A breeze flicked
       grass heads against my shins
       and shivered my sleeves.

On the far side of the bay
       rocks basked,
       and along them a line of gulls
       stood watch, shuffled,
       stood witness.

Somewhere
       in that sky-filled space
       there were voices.

I yelled – Can you hear this?
       I shouted a poem
       into the air.

Your voice
        called, Yes!
        and back came a poem
        over the water.

Only the gulls:
        webbed feet on boulders,
        wind in the feathers,

and all over the sky
        light
        breaking open like eggshells.

On not seeing a fernbird
in the ecosanctuary

Shush. Look there.

> *Surprise. The way a poem shifts …*

Our guide has heard
a rare bird's call
where long grass, fern and bracken reveal
long grass, fern and bracken.

> *the way meaning can be shy …*

They were here, already here, he says,
so near the houses, cats,
rats, in spite of chainsaws
before the pest-proof fence.

> *but persists, leaves secret marks …*

Then we are deep in lushness of tūī,
bellbird, kererū. With wing-beat,
song, they proclaim: Here I am
and see, I am beautiful.

the way a poem sings, so in the gaps
                    between the words …

Back at the top we are quiet
over coffee. At our feet,
the forest canopy,
the long curve of the gully;

on the horizon the Silver Peaks,
distance making the ridge lines
bold, shadows simple,
our eyes drawn to the shine of surface.

                    but then … the way that a poem …

Breakfast song of sparrows

Punctual in the early light,
they gather in the pear tree;

their agitated white noise
of high-pitched cold and hunger,

pushes at the window, insists, insists
on custom and the moral force of winter.

So, I stand beneath the tree,
toss breadcrumbs.

Above my head, sun catches their impatience,
the up and down skipping through the branches

like fingertips that pluck the strings,
an instrument with one note,

repeats, repeats: We need
to eat. Please leave.

At the crib in July

No one's been here for months.
But it's not quite empty.
When you unlock the door you can smell
that Frost is here, the winter squatter.

He's claimed the towels, the sheets,
and wrapped his fingers round the mugs.
You light the fire, boil the jug,
fill the fridge with food, and turn it on.

At night, the room is filled with firelight
and radio, with the whispered percussion
of flames, with a cello that moans love
to the claret in your fire-lit glass.

Frost presses his stare to the blank,
black windows. He's a shiver from ancient
memory, marks out a perimeter: the outside that creates
the inside. Fire, music, you. Another sip.

Alive

Fist.

Hard.

A mind fails
to duck. Stumbles.

Front door
slammed
accelerator
floored.

Has he gone?

Inside the room, no sound.
No movement.
On the table the remote
control points at the screen.
Blank.
The mud-grey surface gleams as if water
has seeped to the lowest
point, and there, the reflection
of the woman on the couch.

The air hangs bruised,
swollen; the walls too tight,
the mud-person bloodless
inside the glass square. The dull
pulse of days like damp clods falling.

Clod falling

clod

clod.

Does she breathe?

Are there gaps between compacted
layers of grief where

breath might reach a cell of rebellion
that persists persists

with pick and crowbar
and muffled dynamite blasts

till the day when a cold
draught gives hint of an exit?

Is there one part of herself
that prepares ropes hooks

a first aid kit
then urgent

shouts her own name
into the dark?

And does she hear in that call
a throat-deep rasp-rough

beginning of song?

Yes.

We are the rule-breakers

We are the rule-breakers, your grandmothers
who lurk in the forest to swallow the wolf.
Big mouths.
Talked about. Never in
the narrative.

We are the rule-breakers, your stepmothers;
against the grain, we follow the bird crumbs
to find you safe,
bring you home.
Never mentioned. As if not in
the family.

We're your aunties under the Tree
of the Knowledge of Good
and Evil. Eat up, we say,
as we munch on our apples.
Big mouths. Full mouths.
Talked about. Never in
the holy books.

But our dance steps are holy
and slightly off-
balance because of exuberance
under our skirts – you, being born,
flying in from the dark: our brave
clever daughters, our wild
gentle sons. You come toothless, wrinkled.
Beautiful.

And see? We're beautiful too with that look
in our eyes that we get from swallowing wolves
and possibly pythons – gaps
in our teeth and foreheads like
untidy knitting. Never on
the magazine covers.

We are the rule-breakers, standing against
every venom-tongued wind.
Broad backs.
Never tamed. Always in
your mirror.

Hut

If I come back as a building
it will be as a tramping hut.

I'll perch at the end
of a hard day, alert as a musterer's dog,
watching for the pack-horse bob of your heads.

Inside, you'll dance the sidestep shuffle
of cramped space, an unreasonable
amount of room being taken by fireplace. Wood
will be stacked round the back.

While your socks and boots steam,
I'll offer you a broad doorstep to sit on. Cold.
Hard on your bums. But worth it because

I'll give you

sky. And ridgelines in long folds
upon folds of wilderness to the planet's edge
and over, where the sun unfurls inventions of orange,
wild pinks and gold. From your centres
of gravity you'll feel the earth turn. Then when the night
is star-spilled and reaching, the chill
will send you in to the fire.

I'll give you

shadows. You'll be encircled
and stroked, till each is opened
to thoughts you never knew you had,
to words you shape with slow carefulness.
From corners that shelter spiders and mice

tenderness will creep. It will unlock in each a sanctum
where another can place her own fragile
flames. Silence will sit with knees in the warmth,
time unmeasured except for
the tick, click of wood's transmutation to ash.

The fire will subside with
flutter, snuffle, settle of embers.

Then I will give you

a morepork.

Far.

Clear.

A potato sonnet:
Jersey Bennes for Christmas

They gleam in the black
crumbled earth;

steady, as if candles
glow through layers of silk,

underpin the season's quick
shifts of tinselled light

and the brisk heel-tap, chatter
of crowds in the street.

This is old, wondrous
as moonrise,

mundane
as the maternal voice

that calls, come in
to the table.

Into a bowl

Measure warm water.
Sprinkle yeast, sugar.
Add oil.
Wait.

On long, quiet, uncommitted days I bake bread.
I do it for the long and the quiet more than food.
For enchantment. After ten minutes in the sun the
yeast forms muddy scum on the water like the first
self-replicating soup, like a gob of mythological
spit that gives life to the clay.

Stir in the warmed flour.
Knead till smooth.
Wait.

As I knead, my knuckles and the heels of my hands
indent the dough like prints in an ancient mud,
petal-soft round the toes. The feet walked on. But
we know they walked by their prints. In another
place, rocks bear 30 thousand-year-old traces of
the grinding of grain. Intimations of bread.

A little salt. Knead and
shape the dough.
Wait.

Wheat, rice, maize changed us. They were part of the recipe for civilisation: take grain, sow, harvest, build an oven, a house, a city. The iceman from the Copper Age had grain in his stomach. An Iron Age man preserved by peat had eaten charred bread as his last meal.

Bend into the heat
from the oven; place the tray
in the centre.
Wait.

The smell of bread baking fills the cavities of the house, of the body. It says: Stand still, breathe deep. It insists that mouths be moist and ready.

Set plates on the table.
Bring in extra chairs.
Time curves from then to here and back.
Now.

First rain after drought

Wait, just wait
for arrival, the quick
kiss, kiss, kiss through
my gateway,
rhododendron leaves' tentative clapping.
Is it here? Here to stay?
Yes. My whole garden sits up.

It's as if the cast of a glittering blockbuster
has deigned to drop by –
sashays through our streets
elegant, larger than life,
distributing fingertip touch,
tardiness never mentioned,
while we ordinary ones open our faces
and shine.

Question: Here is the news. Discuss.

Answer: Are we then, like water?

Drop after insistent drop,
you rattling roofing iron,
me tripping up windscreen wipers –
Listen! Listen! It's important!

A-flash down gutters
breaking over empty cans
catching light in strips
like shredded paper,
speech notes,
ripped and chucked away –

Please answer, answer!
The words baffled, leached, battered
through cacophonous drains
to fall

        why

                  even

                            try

into harbour.

Late afternoon.
Held by green
reflected hills, the water
lifts up children swimming.

Brave as only the young are brave,
small fluid densities of kick and splash and dive,
they send circles, large, larger,
to lap against unknowable near, unknowable far.

The swimmers' mouths open for air,
open, shut, open, like valves of the heart.

The promise of dusk.
Again the rain falls,
on sea, on skin,

first touch:
kiss.

The price of oil

After listening to a 2005 radio interview with Britain's former ambassador to Uzbekistan.

I'm writing a song with no music.
    Not even
    the thrumming and lilt of petrol filling my
    echoing tank.
    It's full now. Tune finished.

I'm writing a song with no singing.
    The man in this photo is dead.
    Boiled alive to force open
    his words, for secrets, for names,
    to sing for President Karimov.

I'm writing a song for the nameless.
    In a courtroom, a witness stands up.
    He can't look at the two young men in the dock.
    In a low voice, 'It's true, these men are terrorists, friends
    of bin Laden. I should know because I'm their uncle.'
    Then, burdened by courage and love: 'No. Not true.
    They tortured my children till I agreed to what they asked.
    But we're no one, just farmers. What do we know
    of bin Laden?'

I'm writing a song about these names:
     Tony Blair, re-elected.
     Jack Straw, re-elected.
     George Bush, re-elected.
     The Uzbekistan president sends his best wishes.
     'What more can I do for you?' Karimov asks them.
     'What more?'

     'My report was naïve,' the ambassador said.
     'I thought they didn't know.'
     And so he was sacked.
     A diplomat's task: to say nothing.
     So nothing. Then nothing and nothing.

I'm writing a song about silence.

Downpour

It never rains but it
spills the ocean
back to the ocean
primal exultation
of water
streaming away and again
to the centre.

It never rains but
the planet's remade
by the slow sculpting
of crag and ravine
surgical shock
of a landslip – raw tide
over old strata.

It never rains but
someone (is it you?)
steps out in the deluge
nostrils awash
eye sockets like ponds
scant memory deeper than bone
of scales fins and gills
slick-headed eel
in blue gumboots
standing in homage.

Planting cabbages

To prepare, you might read some books, or poke your head
over the back fence to watch. Ask.
At the plant shop choose seedlings that look glad to see you.
No shyness, no sulks. The best plants to take home are dancers.

Show them their warm bed where you've worked to make
the soil fine, dark as coffee grounds, and in it
dig holes for them the depth of a cupped human hand.
Imagine how they'll be, high, wide, kingly
with ample curling collars round the head, and allow space
for all that majesty. Plan largesse among your neighbours.

This is all about promises. Promise them rain. And because
they can trust you, let water trickle to turn the soil that receives
them to silken mud, and keep it flowing to stroke
the roots down, into place. Alignment.
Then see how they bounce and flutter in the breeze, amazed
at themselves, like infants on stage at the end-of-year concert.

And you. Socks a bit wet, dirt on your knees
and under your nails. You smell of damp earth.

The punishment of Rona

The name
of the woman in the moon
is Rona.
She knows that she used to be young, knows
that once she lived
among trees.
Now she circles with her back
bent and draws pictures
of birds in the dust.

Once, she was wild with a voice that spun
accusations like cluster bombs,
like shrapnel, like home-made nail bombs
in suicide cars. Other voices fell,
leaked into the grass. This memory
is misted now.

She dreams she walks
on the earth. Young men admire
her translucent skin, bones
like shadows, like the branches
of trees fallen from cliffs to lie
in deep water. She dreams
she is thirsty.
She goes down through the trees
to the creek.

She is carrying water. It will spill.
She knows it will spill.
She wakes
with a mouth
open and empty of words.

At night she looks down where the lights
of the cities lean in together
and point.

Beacon fire

An image has snagged itself in my mind.
It is making demands of me.

A night sky. Stars. Against these
the dark presence of the hill
you and I have known all our lives.
From early morning we've been carrying wood
to the top. And all day, as we picked splinters
from our palms, we have watched
another hill along the coast where the land curves
into the unknown.

Is this memory? A fragment of ancestor
still in the blood?

Then just as we think about sleep,
that hill flings fire to the sky
and there's shouting. We have prepared
the torch. Our own beacon fire stutters
then opens its throat. For a moment
we stare at our hill. We have never seen it
so urgent. A repeating
repeating of hills, but we're too busy to look.
Children, still curled with sleep
are blanket-bundled into carts to send them away
from the coast. Most of the food goes with them.

Is it something I've read? A novel? A history?

We are left, the grown-ups. We pace, we sharpen,
we wait. Then the moment we stand, walk out
to face the thunderous oncoming.
I'm aware of your shoulder.
I hear your attempt to calm
your breathing. I try to calm mine
and fail. But there are so many of us, so many of
us.

Or could this be from the future? There will
be a child. One of ours. Her voice swept back
by storm, by rising tide, does she use mind,
splinter, fire, to cry out?

After the art gallery

I walk
down the street with rectangular
eyes.

Naked tree branches break
glass and stone
to diminishing pieces,
hold them aloft. They sway;
they fit
in delicate miracle.

Outside a café two men
are laughing, ease back
at the waist; the light leans
towards them, the road curves
away. They are beautiful,
beautiful.

Here
in the parking-building –
quiet.
Lines of white, concrete pillars
measure white space, clear room
on the floor for
long parallelograms
of sun that promise
to move. But not yet.

Under-lit, bubbles
of metal hover
in patterns
of broken uniformity.

I open one up and
drive it away.

Skydiving

Awake on the beach,
her sleeping bag scratchy
with heat, salt, sand –
her heavy eyes
surprised
by the oceanic blaze of stars,
the whirl and pull of constellations,
vertigo.

Rolls over, sleeps.

Now, a shift
in the balance.
'Don't fall,'
her children say. 'Be careful –
get a walking stick.'
She won't.

But the years
are faster,
gravity fiercer.
The skydive that began in the birth canal,
illusion of flight,
plunging toward hard fact.

Sleepless by the back door,
there'll be a frost tonight –
the stars so close
over the hedge
like a fine knitted shawl
in place, and ready to catch.
Her scalp prickles with cold
and distance,
as if her fontanelle
is open.

The Catlins

We are not at
the edge
of the world.

Angled, the campervans needlepoint
the margins of the car park. The track drops
to the beach through vertical bush.
We won't tip. Not toward dark ocean trenches.
Not headlong.

The tide recedes, recedes,
rolls out the shining
unreachable.
In the chilled and sunlit sky, the moon is thin
as a misplaced button.

Look behind at the marks we have made
in the sand. Like the work
of a sewing machine losing
its screws. Our footprints stitch,
stitch into the cave,

and out and around
in desultory circles. We zip
up our jackets against wind
that whispers its fable
of ice.

From the back of the cave
blindness stares out.
We take photos.

Dormant

A hot nor'wester blew today
and the cat wandered
through the house complaining
but no one could relieve her
of her thick
black coat.

Now she sleeps in a chair
in the bright yellow chair
with the red satin cushion
where she might
ignite
flare
collapse into ash

so near
the wide-open window

a torch-throated breeze.

Dragons on George Street

We're a carload of old women driving
home through the bright lights of George Street.
It's late on a Saturday night
about half past ten.

The crowds are young and spilling along
the footpaths sparking into the traffic and out,
the light catching upturned faces in the flow
like bubbles in a glass of champagne.

Out there on the street the mood is triumphal
all of them on their way out of the humdrum
as if each one holds high the banner,
the brave fluorescence of being young.

And we know it so well, this banner:
its heraldic trumpets, unicorns, taiaha,
and tassels flinging up to the stars
pushing the moon out of the way.

The lights turn red and we joke
of our own nights as bold standard bearers;
we're encyclopaedic
about what can go wrong.

Do we warn them? With fog horn,
distress flare? Hazard lights?
Run up a skull and crossbones
in the Octagon?

The three-eyed sentinels wink, turn green,
and we're quiet; our laughter's for us
not for them. At their time it's right
to leap astride unicorns.

At our time we're stepping with care.
Old dragons couchant, watchful,
protective. Our eyes are less on the stars,
more on the spaces between.

Making up the spare beds
for the Brothers Grimm

They'll arrive before dark.
So she has aired the mattresses and used a stiff
brush to dislodge peas, spiders, frogs that lurk.
She has opened the windows and spread
sheets over the beds between layers of sunshine. The room
smells of linen crisped by the wind.

What can she offer them? Not true love, though she's heard
that a young man looking for love was given
a bowl of milk, a chunk of white bread
and a freshly minted coin that sparkled.
She has kneaded the bread, set it in the hot oven.

Are their lives soft with luxury? She can't give
them that, though she's heard that while searching
for fortune, a traveller was given an ordinary
stone from the side of the road.
He was advised: Use it, hit it as hard as you can
and straighten out your old nails.

She's acquainted with stones; there are three
by the back door and she knows their moments of stirring
when hibernation grows wakeful. Do they sleep
because they're bewitched, or have they made solemn vows?
Might a stone break its word? And what then?

The stains are still there. She checks the cracks
in the walls where the red seeps through. Scrubbing
with soap and cold water helps till the trickle
comes back. She pushes the beds to hide the worst
marks.

She brings extra blankets. Snow is forecast for later.
This is the room where weeping lives in the darkness,
like a child, soft, surreptitious. If the weather
keeps its word the sound will be gathered in by
the moans of the midnight wind. But the light
in the hallway – she could leave it switched on.

The pillows are soft with invitation. They speak of trust.
A blue coverlet, a green coverlet. She stands back. Sighs.
Then she makes coffee and looks at the clock.
The brothers are late.

Falling asleep

Tonight the wind is blowing steady from the north-east.
Your walls hum.
It feels as if your whole house is stowed in the cargo hold
of some huge aircraft, engines muted through your floor.

*Current speed: the galaxy and you, travel at 3,600,000
kilometres per hour through the universe.*

You pull down a blind
and your fire murmurs in the log burner
which must break some regulation
about air cargo.

*Current speed: the solar system and you, travel at 675,000
kilometres per hour around the galaxy.*

You wonder if it's too late for coffee
as the ancient physics of earth and sky are revving
pushing, testing the bricks of your chimney.
It cradles the inside. Here in this quiet cabin space
you're drowsy, lulled, lulled by the journey.

*Current speed: the planet and you, travel at 107,000
kilometres per hour around the sun.*

You imagine sunlight,
imagine aircraft wings approaching bright cloud
towering, half-sculpted as if you're in Michelangelo's mind,
his thoughts
still in flow, still searching.

*Current speed: the world with you, rotates at 1,610
kilometres per hour into the night.*

Hush. Switches are flicked.
Calculation: off.
Attentiveness: off.
Your eyes won't stay open.

There's a lullaby in the wind tonight
a rocking song of vastness, song of the black
hole of ceasing to be, into which you fall
with the trust of a baby.
Held in the core. Until morning.

The time of fire is over

Streaked with iron oxide,
with old, spilled blood,
the horizon's lower than you thought, hushed.
But its turning's undiminished.
It spins you until centrifugal force sends eyes,
mouth, ears off on wild, independent travel.

       Your feet stand firm,
              align themselves.

Only your hands return broken, to fly
in circles, endless faltering circles.
You know your skin is growing brittle,
ill-fitting; if it fails your knees won't bend
for the remnants. You knew that some hours ago.

       Your feet balance,
              step experimentally.

All around you now the air,
voluminous, pushes,
sways with invisible parachutes.

       Your toes curl, grasp
              the edge.

Notes & acknowledgements

Old possumers' track. Ngiru-ngiru is the southern Māori name for the bird known further north as miro miro or tit.

The punishment of Rona. From a Māori/Polynesian myth. In some traditions Rona is female, in others male.

THANKS TO the editors of the following publications where some of these poems, or versions of them, have appeared: *Deep South, Landfall, Otago Daily Times, Critic, Takahē, Poems in the Waiting Room, Poetry New Zealand*.

And thanks to the New Zealand Poetry Society, Caselberg Trust, and Poems in the Waiting Room, for organising the competitions where some of my poems were singled out for prize or mention, and the NZ Society of Authors' appraisal service and the encouraging appraisal of an early version of this collection by Sue Fitchett.

For inspiration and support, I am grateful to Dunedin's poetry community, my poetry group – especially Martha Morseth and Cy Mathews – and to the poets of Upfront and the Octagon Collective. Special thanks are due to artist Claire Beynon for the cover image, and for all the brainstorming and meticulous work on the way, and to Mary McCallum of Mākaro Press for her perceptiveness and care with my poems.

Finally thanks to my Dad who gave me a childhood filled with poetry.

HO●PLA SERIES

HOOPLA entices people to buy and read poetry books through the quality of its poets, the attraction of a series with three books launching at once, vibrant design and the accessibility of a clear narrative or theme. We like strong work that steps onto the tightrope without hesitation and gives the performance of its life. It's no accident the word 'Hoopla' has connotations of commotion, extravagance and play about it. Hoopla books are published annually in April in sets of three. A new poet joins a mid-career and a late-career poet.

2015

Mr Clean & The Junkie Jennifer Compton • VICE/HOOPLA

A 70s love story which begins at a Sydney casino and ends in a remote river valley in northern New Zealand. An Elvis Costello lookalike and the son of a local crime boss, Jon is on his way to the casino to launder a briefcase of his father's cash when he catches sight of gambling junkie, Justine.

Native bird Bryan Walpert • SETTLER/HOOPLA

BRYAN WALPERT – who arrived here from the United States a decade ago – writes of what it's been like to be an observer or 'birdwatcher' in a land whose physical and cultural geographies he is still learning to name.

Bones in the Octagon Carolyn McCurdie • SOUTH/HOOPLA

2014

Heart absolutely I can Michael Harlow • LOVE/HOOPLA

Cinema Helen Rickerby • FILM/HOOPLA

Bird murder Stefanie Lash • CRIME/HOOPLA

www.makaropress.co.nz